Hello! I like to hide.

This is Helen.

2

This is Conor.

5

This is Mammy.

I like to hide from Daddy.

This is Daddy.

8

q

This is Gran.

11

This is Jill.

13

This is Rex.   This is Tabby.

Mammy and Daddy and Gran

Helen and Jill and Conor

Rex and Tabby and Bunny

Goodbye!